TIMELINE *of the* VIETNAM WAR

By Charlie Samuels

Please visit our website, www.garethstevens.com. For a free color catalog of all our high-quality books, call toll free 1-800-542-2595 or fax 1-877-542-2596.

Library of Congress Cataloging-in-Publication Data
Samuels, Charlie, 1961-
Timeline of the Vietnam War / Charlie Samuels.
     p. cm. — (Americans at war: a Gareth Stevens timeline series)
Includes index.
ISBN 978-1-4339-5920-2 (pbk.)
ISBN 978-1-4339-5921-9 (6-pack)
ISBN 978-1-4339-5918-9 (library binding)
1. Vietnam War, 1961-1975—Juvenile literature. 2. Vietnam War, 1961-1975—Chronology—Juvenile literature. 3. Vietnam War, 1961-1975—United States—Juvenile literature. I. Title.
DS557.7.S26 2011
959.704'3—dc22

2011003041

Published in 2012 by
Gareth Stevens Publishing
111 East 14th Street, Suite 349
New York, NY 10003

© 2012 Brown Bear Books Ltd.

For Brown Bear Books Ltd:
Editorial Director: Lindsey Lowe
Managing Editor: Tim Cooke
Children's Publisher: Anne O'Daly
Art Director: Jeni Child
Designer: Karen Perry
Picture Manager: Sophie Mortimer
Production Director: Alastair Gourlay

Picture Credits:
Front Cover: Library of Congress/Robert Hunt Library

Key: t = top, b = bottom
Robert Hunt Library: 6, 7, 8, 9, 11, 12, 22, 29, 35, 37t, 37b, 42, 44, 45t, 45b; **U.S. National Archives:** 10, 13, 14, 15, 16, 17, 18, 19, 20t, 20b, 21, 24, 25t, 25b, 26, 28t, 28b, 30, 31, 32, 33, 34, 36, 38, 40, 41, 43

All Artworks Brown Bear Books Ltd.

Publisher's note to educators and parents: Our editors have carefully reviewed the websites that appear on p. 47 to ensure that they are suitable for students. Many websites change frequently, however, and we cannot guarantee that a site's future contents will continue to meet our high standards of quality and educational value. Be advised that students should be closely supervised whenever they access the Internet.

All rights reserved. No part of this book may be reproduced, stored in a retrieval system, or transmitted in any form or by any means, electronic, mechanical, photocopying, recording, or otherwise, without the prior written permission of the copyright holder.

Manufactured in the United States of America
1 2 3 4 5 6 7 8 9   12 11 10

CPSIA compliance information: Batch #BRS11GS: For further information contact Gareth Stevens, New York, New York at 1-800-542-2595.

Contents

Introduction	4
Causes of the War	6
The War Escalates	10
An American War	14
A Year of Hard Fighting	18
Khe Sanh	22
Tet Offensive	26
The Death Toll Mounts	30
Operation Rolling Thunder	34
Cambodia	38
End Game	42
Glossary	46
Further Reading	47
Index	48

Introduction

The Vietnam War was already old when the United States become actively involved in 1963; it would last another 12 years and cost 50,000 US lives.

An independence campaign led by the Viet Minh had split the French colony of Vietnam into two countries in 1946: communist North Vietnam, backed by China and the Soviet Union, and the French-sponsored Republic of Vietnam.

The Course of the War

The reason the war was not simply a local conflict lay in the strategic struggles of the Cold War. US politicians feared the spread of Soviet communism. The so-called domino theory suggested that if one country in a region became communist, others would follow. When North Vietnamese military action forced a French withdrawal from Vietnam, therefore, the Americans chose to step in. They began by sending advisors to help the Army of the Republic of Vietnam (ARVN), but their military presence quickly grew as fighting broke out. The main clashes came near the demilitarized zone (DMZ), or "no-man's land." There was also extensive guerrilla warfare in the South, conducted by the Viet Cong, an underground army. Facing a determined enemy, rising casualty figures, and increasing protests at home, the United States transferred responsibility for fighting to its South Vietnamese allies and had withdrawn its troops before the final fall of the South in April 1975.

About This Book

This book contains two types of timelines. Along the bottom of the pages is a timeline that covers the whole period. It lists key events and developments, color coded to indicate events in the land and air campaigns or in the political field. Each chapter also has its own timeline, which runs vertically down the sides of the pages. This timeline gives more specific details about the particular subject of the chapter.

Soldiers of the 4th Infantry Division take cover at the edge of a field during an operation in October 1967.

Causes of the War

What began as an attempt to shore up a friendly regime in South Vietnam escalated from 1965 into a military test of will for the United States and the most divisive issue of the age.

Viet Minh independence fighters take possession of Haiphong in 1955 after the withdrawal of the French.

Timeline 1950–1963

March 20, 1954 United States US leaders discuss helping the French in Indochina, where French forces are besieged at Dien Bien Phu.

1950 — 1955

KEY:
- Land war
- Air war
- Politics

May 7, 1954 North Vietnam Dien Bien Phu falls to the Viet Minh, Vietnamese independence fighters.

January 1, 1955 South Vietnam The first US military advisors arrive in South Vietnam.

Vietnam in Southeast Asia occupies part of the Southeast Asian peninsula formerly known as Indochina, which also includes Thailand, Myanmar (Burma), Laos, and Cambodia.

The Europeans Arrive

The first Europeans to arrive in Indochina were French Catholic priests in the 17th century. By the 19th century, local rulers wanted to get rid of them and their influence on local people. But the French government protected the priests and sent warships to the area to threaten the local rulers. In 1862, Emperor Tu Duc of Vietnam was forced to sign a treaty with France that protected the priests and gave France the right to trade in the area.

The French Take Over

Over the next 20 years, the French sent more people to the region. Indochina was rich in gold, silver, spices, and other precious goods, which the French wanted to control. By 1887, they

Timeline

March 6, 1946 Ho Chi Minh signs an agreement with the French that recognizes him as president of the Democratic Republic of Vietnam (later called North Vietnam). The French set up a separate state in the South.

December 19, 1946 War breaks out between the French and North Vietnam.

March 20, 1954 American leaders discuss helping the French in Indochina. French forces are surrounded at Dien Bien Phu.

May 7, 1954 Dien Bien Phu falls to the Viet Minh. The French have lost 35,000 men in the war and are forced to leave Vietnam.

January 1, 1955 US military advisors arrive in South Vietnam.

(continued, page 8)

⇐ John F. Kennedy escalated US involvement in South Vietnam.

August 2, 1961 United States President John F. Kennedy commits the United States to supporting South Vietnam.

November 22, 1963 United States President Kennedy is assassinated in Dallas.

1960

January 1958 South Vietnam North Vietnam decides to launch a takeover of South Vietnam.

January 2, 1963 South Vietnam ARVN (South Vietnamese) soldiers, supplied by the United States, suffer defeat at Ap Bac.

November 24, 1963 United States New president Lyndon B. Johnson vows to continue US support for South Vietnam.

The Vietnam War

Timeline (continued)

January 1958 North Vietnam begins a campaign to conquer South Vietnam. It orders communist guerrillas operating in South Vietnam to begin the attack.

December 1960 North Vietnam forms the Viet Cong (Vietnamese communists) to fight in South Vietnam.

August 2, 1961 President Kennedy announces that the United States will help South Vietnam.

February 7, 1962 There are now 4,000 US military personnel in South Vietnam, training the South's soldiers.

May 16, 1962 President Kennedy announces that troops will be sent to protect neighboring Thailand.

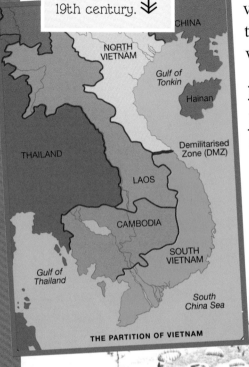

France ruled Indochina in the 19th century.

THE PARTITION OF VIETNAM

ruled most of Indochina and had decided to incorporate the peninsula into their empire. By the end of the century, around 50,000 French people lived there. Local people were treated as second-class citizens and were very poor. They rose up against the French, but their rebellions were crushed.

Ho Chi Minh

Japan conquered Indochina during World War II but was forced to leave after its defeat in 1945. Communists in Vietnam, led by Ho Chi Minh, seized power. Ho declared himself president in August 1945.

French troops watch reinforcements parachute into Dien Bien Phu.

Timeline
1964 January–December

February 7 South Vietnam A Viet Cong bomb explodes in a Saigon theater, killing three Americans and wounding 50.

January   April

KEY:

 Land war

 Air war

Politics

April 25 South Vietnam General William C. Westmoreland takes charge of Military Assistance Command in Vietnam (MACV).

Causes of the War

In October, French troops arrived to reclaim the country. They captured the South, but in March 1946, the French recognized Ho Chi Minh as president of a new communist country in the North: the Democratic Republic of Vietnam. The French created a new country in the South, later known as the Republic of Vietnam. War broke out in December 1946 as the two sides fought for control of the whole country. The French lost and withdrew, but by then the South Vietnamese had a new supporter: the United States.

Ho Chi Minh led the North Vietnamese war effort.

The United States

US politicians were concerned that the loss of one country to communism would create a "domino effect" in which neighboring states would also fall to communism. On August 2, 1961, President John F. Kennedy announced that the United States would do all it could to support South Vietnam and save it from communist takeover. He sent in more military personnel, initially to act as advisors.

Dien Bien Phu

The turning point in the war between North Vietnam and the French was the siege of Dien Bien Phu. The French set up a base there in late 1953 behind enemy lines in North Vietnam. The North Vietnamese surrounded it in March 1954 and began a seige. The French were unable to get supplies in to the stronghold, and on May 7 they surrendered. Some 2,200 of the 16,000 troops had died in the siege.

August 5 North Vietnam US aircraft bomb North Vietnam in retaliation for the attack in Gulf of Tonkin.

October South Vietnam Some 1,300 US special forces, the Green Berets, arrive.

November 3 United States Lyndon B. Johnson is elected president of the United States.

August → October →

August 2 Gulf of Tonkin North Vietnamese torpedo boats attack USS *Maddox* in the Gulf of Tonkin; President Johnson warns that the United States will defend itself.

August 5 United States Congress approves the Southeast Asia Resolution, allowing any steps to be taken to protect US personnel within Vietnam.

November South Vietnam A North Vietnamese attack wins control of much of Binh Dinh province in South Vietnam.

The War Escalates

As the political situation in South Vietnam worsened, it became clear that the United States' involvement would have to increase and more troops would be required.

Three Viet Cong fighters → stand on top of a captured ARVN M113 armored personnel carrier.

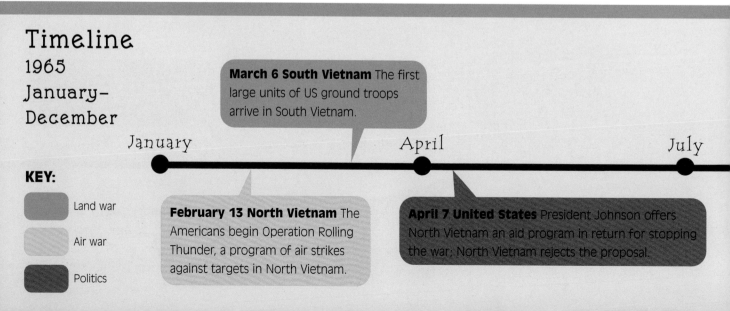

Timeline
1965 January–December

KEY:
- Land war
- Air war
- Politics

March 6 South Vietnam The first large units of US ground troops arrive in South Vietnam.

February 13 North Vietnam The Americans begin Operation Rolling Thunder, a program of air strikes against targets in North Vietnam.

April 7 United States President Johnson offers North Vietnam an aid program in return for stopping the war; North Vietnam rejects the proposal.

The War Escalates

The political situation inside South Vietnam was deteriorating. President Ngo Dinh Diem faced both a liberation campaign waged by Viet Cong (VC) communist guerrillas and growing dissatisfaction from the Buddhists who made up the bulk of the population. The South Vietnamese army (with American approval) launched a coup d'état (revolt) against the president and his brother, both of whom were killed in the first week of November 1963.

US Troops Arrive

Despite political instability in the South, the growing strength of the North and the inauguration of Lyndon B. Johnson as the new US president saw the United States increase its military support to South Vietnam. By the end of 1964, the United States Military Assistance Command, Vietnam (MACV), under General William C. Westmoreland, had grown to more than 20,000 men.

In 1964, the US marines contingent in Vietnam numbered

This Viet Cong recruit wears typical clothing and carries a mortar stand.

Timeline

January 2, 1963 ARVN soldiers, equipped by the United States, suffer a humiliating defeat at the hands of the Viet Cong at Ap Bac.

July 17, 1963 South Vietnamese police put down a protest by 1,000 Buddhists.

November 1, 1963 Military coup in South Vietnam; President Diem is shot dead the next day.

August 2, 1964 North Vietnamese torpedo boats attack the USS *Maddox* in the Gulf of Tonkin.

August 5, 1964 US aircraft bomb North Vietnam in retaliation for *Maddox* attack.

November 1964 Viet Cong and NVA regiments take control of most of Binh Dinh province in South Vietnam; ARVN forces are destroyed or pushed back.

(continued, page 12)

September 18 South Vietnam US aircraft begin to attack Viet Cong positions.

October 14 United States The US Defense Department orders a military draft call for 45,224 men.

November 4 South Vietnam The Battle of the Ia Drang Valley sees heavy losses for both sides.

November 27 South Vietnam The South Vietnamese army suffers a major defeat in battle at the Michelin Rubber Plantation.

December 15 North Vietnam The US Air Force bombs and destroys a North Vietnamese power plant, the first raid on a major industrial target.

12 The Vietnam War

Timeline (continued)

February 13, 1965 Americans start Operation Rolling Thunder, a program of air attacks against North Vietnam.

September 18, 1965 1st Brigade, 101st Airborne Division, begins operations in Son Con Valley; the Viet Cong are badly damaged.

October 19, 1965 NVA opens its campaign against the Americans.

November 4, 1965 The Battle of the Ia Drang Valley lasts for 35 days; the US 1st Cavalry Division suffers heavy casualties.

November 27, 1965 South Vietnamese army suffers a major defeat in battle at the Michelin Rubber Plantation.

December 15, 1965 First US air raid on North Vietnamese industrial target—a power plant at Uongbi is hit.

more than 800 men. The majority were located in South Vietnam's I Corps Tactical Zone (ICTZ), closest to the so-called demilitarized zone (DMZ), a narrow strip of no-man's land bordering North Vietnam.

After a clash in the Gulf of Tonkin in August 1964, the United States became drawn into ground fighting, and President Johnson ordered air strikes against targets in North Vietnam in Operation Rolling Thunder. After South Vietnamese army units suffered a series of defeats on the ground, the US Joint Chiefs of Staff approved sending more US marines to South Vietnam.

US air power became crucial to the support of ground units.

Timeline 1966 January–December

April 24 South Vietnam The first major Allied move into enemy territory since 1962 discovers vast quantities of supplies close to Cambodian border.

January ———————————— April ———————————— July

KEY:
- Land war
- Air war
- Politics

January 4 South Vietnam The Viet Cong use Soviet 120-mm mortars, the heaviest weapon used by them so far, at Khe Sanh.

July 7–August 2 South Vietnam Operation Hastings is the largest military action to date.

Full-Scale War

By the end of 1965, the war in Vietnam had become an American war. More than 148,300 combat and support troops had been sent to South Vietnam. Their allies, the Army of the Republic of Vietnam (ARVN), had 500,000 men in 1965, rising to one million in the 1970s. Many of its officers were corrupt and poorly motivated, however. In contrast, the 400,000 troops of the North Vietnamese Army (NVA), were well trained, well led, and had high morale.

Inside South Vietnam, the VC were at least 10,000 strong in 1965. Nicknamed "Charlie" by the Americans, most VC guerrillas were recruited in the South, but received weapons, reinforcements, and guidance from North Vietnamese Army soldiers based in the South. The VC fought a guerrilla war of ambush, terrorism, and sabotage, using small units to control villages in the countryside, but leaving the main population centers to government authorities. They were an elusive enemy.

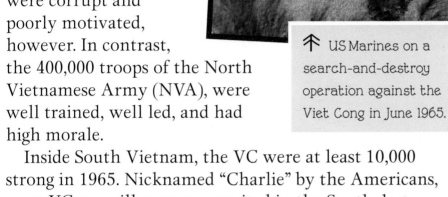

US Marines on a search-and-destroy operation against the Viet Cong in June 1965.

Gulf of Tonkin Incident

On August 2, about 28 miles (45 km) off the North Vietnamese coast in the Gulf of Tonkin, the destroyer USS *Maddox* was attacked by three North Vietnamese gunboats. One was disabled and a second retreated; the third sprayed the *Maddox* with machine-gun fire. On August 4, the *Maddox* and USS *C. Turner Joy* were attacked again by North Vietnamese gunboats. The US ships opened fire, sinking one, and possibly two, North Vietnamese vessels.

September–November South Vietnam Operation Attleboro sees largest number of enemy dead to date, with 1,106 confirmed casualties.

October 25 South Vietnam Operation Thayer I begins; it lasts for 111 days.

October 24–25 The Philippines President Johnson and other leaders issue a Declaration of Peace, but North Vietnam ignores the request for a peaceful end to the war.

November 30 South Vietnam Operation Fairfax begins; it will last 380 days and inflict 1,043 casualties on the Viet Cong.

An American War

By 1966, the war in Vietnam was "America's War." Soldiers, sailors, marines, and airmen fought the Viet Cong and the North Vietnamese Army (NVA).

American troops rest on a bunker. The soldier holds an M79 grenade launcher, often used in jungle firefights.

Timeline
1967 January–December

KEY:
- Land war
- Air war
- Politics

January 8 South Vietnam
US Army launches Operation Cedar Falls to destroy the enemy around Saigon.

February 21 South Vietnam
Operation Junction City attempts to stop the enemy from fleeing into Cambodia.

March 2 South Vietnam
US fighter jets mistakenly bomb Lang Vei village, killing Vietnamese civilians.

March 19 South Vietnam
Viet Cong almost wipe out Fire Support Base Gold, but Americans fight back.

April 24 South Vietnam
A major battle is fought near the Khe Sanh fire base close to North Vietnamese border.

An American War

The Viet Cong and North Vietnamese could not match US firepower or maneuverability, but the growing number of US units in Vietnam did not prevent men and material from North Vietnam entering the South via a secret route known as the Ho Chi Minh Trail. US commanders adopted an aggressive search-and-destroy tactic, sending units into hostile territory to seek the enemy. The communists usually started the fighting when it suited them and broke off combat when they wanted to, however, making the search-and-destroy tactic somewhat ineffective. With 200,000 North Vietnamese males reaching draft age every year, General Westmoreland's aim of wearing down the enemy would never succeed.

Timeline

January 4, 1966 Viet Cong and North Vietnamese Army (NVA) attack a US Special Forces camp using Soviet 120-mm mortars, the heaviest weapon so far used by the North Vietnamese.

March 4–8, 1966 Operation Utah sees US marines and South Vietnamese troops fighting NVA; they lose one-third of troops.

July 7–August 2, 1966 The largest military action of war so far, Operation Hastings, takes place near the DMZ. Over 28 days, US marines and South Vietnamese troops kill more than 882 Viet Cong.

August 1–25, 1966 Operation Paul Revere in Pleiku Province sees 809 communists killed.

(continued, page 16)

← UH-1D helicopters airlift troops during Operation Garfield against the Viet Cong, February 17, 1966.

May 11 South Vietnam First Battle of Khe Sanh ends with North Vietnamese losses at 940 and US losses at 155.

August 27 South Vietnam The Viet Cong launch raids in the Mekong Delta.

November 2 South Vietnam The Viet Cong launch raids on refugee settlements.

December 8 South Vietnam One of the largest battles in Mekong Delta sees Viet Cong beaten.

Timeline (continued)

August 6–21, 1966 Operation Colorado is a combined US Marine Corps and South Vietnamese operation that kills 674 Viet Cong.

September–November, 1966 There are 1,106 communist casualties in Operation Attleboro, the largest number so far killed by US military action.

October 2–24, 1966 Operation Irving is a combined effort of US, South Vietnamese, and Korean troops.

October 25, 1966 Operation Thayer I begins.

November 30, 1966 Operation Fairfax starts. It will last for 380 days.

Soldiers are airlifted by UH-1D helicopters during a search-and-destroy mission.

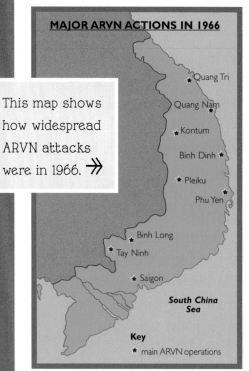

This map shows how widespread ARVN attacks were in 1966.

US Air Force Operations

As 1966 progressed, the US Air Force's (USAF's) Operation Rolling Thunder increased. It saw sustained bombing of North Vietnam and of hostile targets in South Vietnam and along the Laos border.

The US Navy

The US Navy and its South Vietnamese allies patrolled the many rivers and waterways in southern Vietnam and along the country's long coastline. Operation Market Time (a combined US Navy and South Vietnamese navy effort to stop supplies from North Vietnam) soon began to have an effect on the flow of weapons and men reaching the Viet Cong operating in the Mekong Delta in the South.

A Well-Armed Enemy

The year 1966 witnessed a tenfold increase in activity for the US military as it faced a brave and determined enemy. The enemy was

Timeline 1968 January–December

January 30 South Vietnam NVA and Viet Cong launch attacks—the Tet Offensive—across South Vietnam.

January 31 South Vietnam Viet Cong troops hold the US embassy in Saigon for six hours before US troops retake it.

February 23 South Vietnam The siege of Khe Sanh sees heavy shelling by North Vietnamese.

March 16 South Vietnam US troops massacre 300 civilians in the village of My Lai.

May 13 France Peace talks begin in Paris.

July 1 South Vietnam General Creighton Adams replaces General Westmoreland as commander in Vietnam.

KEY:
- Land war
- Air war
- Politics

An American War

↑ A US medical officer treats a woman; such programs aimed to win the trust of the population.

also increasingly well armed. American troops found themselves fighting North Vietnamese Army troops equipped with the AK-47 Kalashnikov assault rifle and RP-2s (rocket-propelled grenade launchers).

Throughout 1966, enemy units were employing superior Soviet-supplied weapons. Viet Cong and NVA sappers launched heavy mortar attacks against the Special Forces camp at Khe Sanh and the Da Nang airfield. Soviet 120-mm heavy mortars allowed the communists to launch attacks throughout the South, thereby increasing the problems of base security.

Tropical Warfare

"Grunts"—US infantry—had to endure terrible conditions. There were 131 species of venomous snakes. In the humid climate, minor cuts did not heal and flesh would rot. In the monsoon, soldiers were soaked to the skin, uniforms chaffing their skin. Tins filled with water as they ate. Trails were mined and booby-trapped with concealed pits full of "punji stakes." These sharpened bamboo spears were often smeared with excrement to cause blood poisoning in anyone who fell on them.

October 31 United States President Johnson announces a complete halt in aerial and naval bombardment of North Vietnam.

December 29 South Vietnam The United States and South Vietnam will no longer honor holiday truces after the Tet Offensive.

October — December

August 23 South Vietnam Communist troops mount their third major offensive this year.

November 5 United States Richard M. Nixon elected president by a narrow margin.

A Year of Hard Fighting

As 1967 arrived, US, South Vietnamese, and Allied forces were locked in a war becoming more intense as more North Vietnamese troops entered the conflict.

The ace of spades on the US helicopter's nose was a deadly omen for Viet Cong troops. →

Timeline
1969 January–June

February 16 South Vietnam Allied forces observe 24-hour cease-fire during the Tet holiday, but the North Vietnamese break it repeatedly.

April 13 South Vietnam US dead in Vietnam reach 33,641, passing the total lost in the Korean War (1950–1953).

January 20 United States Richard M. Nixon is inaugurated as president.

February 27–28 South Vietnam Allied forces find huge supplies of enemy arms during Operation Dewey Canyon.

KEY:
- Land war
- Air war
- Politics

A Year of Hard Fighting

The US and South Vietnamese military carried out ongoing offensives in and along the demilitarized zone (DMZ). Marines in I Corps Tactical Zone started offensives to cut off the infiltration of NVA forces into the Northern and Central Highlands. The leathernecks—the nickname of the US marines—began setting up the "McNamara Line," a series of electronic sensors and warning systems to warn the Allies of enemy movement in border areas. Despite such measures, Hanoi continued to send men and supplies down the Ho Chi Minh Trail. In the South, Viet Cong activity increased as "Charlie" waged war against Saigon and its US backer.

The Highlands and Delta

In the Central Highlands, the US Army went on the offensive and inflicted a series of punishing defeats on the enemy.

The US Navy, meanwhile, kept up the pressure on the North Vietnamese and Viet Cong

Timeline

January 8, 1967 US Army launches Operation Cedar Falls, targeting the Viet Cong in the "Iron Triangle" around Saigon; the US troops seize supplies and destroy enemy positions; many Viet Cong flee.

March 19, 1967 More than 600 Viet Cong die in an attack on Fire Support Base Gold in Operation Junction City.

April 24, 1967 A major battle begins between US marines and the North Vietnamese Army at Khe Sanh fire base close to the North Vietnamese border.

May 11, 1967 First Battle of Khe Sanh ends with 155 marines killed and NVA losses of 940.

(continued, page 20)

← Suspected Viet Cong prisoners await questioning.

May 3 United States The United States offers to withdraw troops if communists reduce their attacks.

May 10 South Vietnam Operation Apache Snow sees heavy losses as U.S. troops capture "Hamburger Hill."

May 12 South Vietnam Viet Cong and NVA launch some of the largest number of attacks since Tet Offensive of 1968.

June 8 United States President Nixon announces the first US troop withdrawals in this increasingly unpopular war.

June →

The Vietnam War

Timeline (continued)

August 13–19, 1967 US B-52 bombers carry out raids on different strategic sites in North Vietnam.

August 27, 1967 The Viet Cong attack South Vietnamese civilians in the Mekong Delta.

November 2, 1967 Viet Cong launch a number of raids against refugee settlements, killing civilians and destroying homes.

December 8, 1967 In a large battle in the Mekong Delta, the South Vietnamese 21st Infantry Division trap Viet Cong, who lose 365 dead.

December 22, 1967 Korean Marine Brigade begins Operation Flying Dragon.

The stress of war: a weary US sailor takes a break on board a navy ship.

US troops search for the enemy in the network of tunnels where they hid.

through its interception campaign in the Mekong Delta and inland waterways south of Saigon. It also provided backup to air attacks.

Air Strikes on the North

The US Air Force maintained steady pressure on the enemy through its three-pronged offensive in the skies over South Vietnam and Laos, and bombing missions against the Ho Chi Minh Trail and petroleum, oil, and lubricants (POL) plants in North Vietnam. It also attacked bridges and major railroads.

Timeline 1969 July–December

August South Vietnam Enemy activity increases throughout Vietnam.

September United States Racial tensions flare between black and white marines.

September 2 North Vietnam Ho Chi Minh, North Vietnam's president, dies of heart failure.

October 15 United States Vietnam Moratoriums, protesting against the war, are held throughout the United States.

KEY:
- Land war
- Air war
- Politics

Increasing US Troop Levels

On the political front, US president Johnson and his advisors struggled to keep the pressure on North Vietnam. The Johnson administration also tried to placate the highly vocal antiwar movement at home. But his attempts failed.

As the war expanded—over 400,000 US troops would be in Vietnam by 1967—so did the size of the antiwar movement at home. For example, in April 1967, more than 300,000 people demonstrated against the war in New York. Six months later, 50,000 protestors surrounded the Pentagon. Within the United States, support for the war was falling: by the autumn of 1967, only 35 percent of Americans supported the war in Vietnam.

International Allies

America was not alone in fighting. In 1967, President Lyndon B. Johnson's "More Flags" campaign asked allies for support. Among those who sent troops were Australia, Thailand, New Zealand, the Philippines, Taiwan, and Spain. The largest number of non-American troops came from South Korea: 48,000 in 1967. Britain's crack SAS regiment is rumored to have helped. Others sent medical supplies.

⇐ In the Mekong Delta, the "brown water" navy patrols the waterways.

November 1 South Vietnam Operation Toan Thang is launched; 5,493 communists will be killed.

December 1 United States The first drawing of the controversial and unpopular draft lottery takes place.

November 13–15 United States An antiwar demonstration is held in Washington, DC.

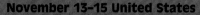

KHE SANH

When its base at Khe Sanh was attacked, the United States responded with heavy firepower; but the commander's strategy later came into question.

US marines wait to be airlifted out of Khe Sanh during the NVA siege, February 22, 1967.

Timeline
1970 January–June

January 21 South Vietnam Communist forces attack US troops near the Cambodian border, across which they then retreat.

February 17 United States President Nixon announces that the South Vietnamese are taking a larger share in fighting, a process known as Vietnamization.

February 5 France At the Paris Peace talks, the North Vietnamese produce a first letter from a US POW held by the Viet Cong.

March 19 Cambodia Prince Norodom Sihanouk is overthrown.

KEY:
- Land war
- Air war
- Politics

KHE SANH

Khe Sanh was a US forward base constructed around a former French airstrip, close to the demilitarized zone. It was near to the border of Laos, straddling Route 9, which was a major infiltration route used by North Vietnamese troops.

In the summer of 1966, US commander General William Westmoreland strengthened the base at Khe Sanh as a springboard for operations into Laos, which President Lyndon B. Johnson later vetoed. Through 1967, in particular between April 24 and May 11, troops of the 3rd Marine Division met the North Vietnamese Army (NVA) in a number of fierce pitched battles in the surrounding hills.

Lessons Learned

In late 1967, US intelligence reports indicated that the enemy was preparing for a major

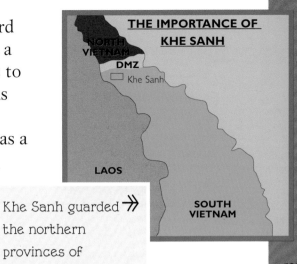

Khe Sanh guarded the northern provinces of South Vietnam.

Timeline

April 24, 1967 Heavy fighting breaks out at Khe Sanh between US marines and the NVA.

May 11, 1967 The battle ends; the 1st Marine Aircraft Wing has flown more than 1,110 sorties, and US marine and army artillery units have fired more than 25,000 rounds at the enemy.

January 20, 1968 Fighting around Hill 881 South near Khe Sanh.

January 21, 1968 The NVA begins to shell Khe Sanh and other Marine Corps outposts on hills around the base; the siege lasts 77 days.

(continued, page 24)

⇐ Westmoreland aimed to draw the NVA into a set-piece battle at Khe Sanh.

April 29 Cambodia US and South Vietnamese forces attack North Vietnamese bases in Cambodia.

April 30 United States There is a public outcry about the attacks in Cambodia.

May 4 United States Campus protests see four students killed by National Guardsmen at Kent State University, Ohio.

June 27 Cambodia The last US and South Vietnamese troops leave Cambodia.

June

The Vietnam War

Timeline (continued)

February 23, 1968 NVA artillery gunners and mortars fire more than 1,300 shells in the heaviest shelling of the siege.

April 1, 1968 1st Air Cavalry Division and units from 1st Marines and ARVN begin Operation Pegasus to relieve the beleaguered garrison.

April 15, 1968 Operation Pegasus ends with the relief and resupply of Khe Sanh; casualties stand at 1,011 enemy dead with 51 marines dead and 459 injured.

June 27, 1968 US marines begin to dismantle the base at Khe Sanh; it is then abandoned.

July 1, 1968 General Creighton Abrams relieves Westmoreland as Commander, US Military Assistance Command, Vietnam.

For close fighting, marines used small arms and flamethrowers. ⇒

attack. In early January 1968, some 40,000 North Vietnamese troops began converging on Khe Sanh. Westmoreland believed that the enemy intended to grab the northernmost provinces of South Vietnam, prior to opening peace negotiations—just as their forerunners had overrun the French base at Dien Bien Phu in 1954 to help improve their bargaining position at the approaching Geneva Peace Conference.

Westmoreland moved 6,000 marines into the area and initiated Operation Niagara, a series of tactical air strikes to break up NVA concentrations. On January 21, the NVA attacked, and the siege of Khe Sanh began.

A Devastating Bombardment

US bombers dropped more than 75,000 tons (68,000 tonnes) of high explosives on NVA formations—the largest aerial assault on a

Timeline
1970 July–December

August 30 South Vietnam Viet Cong attack voters during elections.

July — October

October 8 South Vietnam US commanders complete plans to send home a further 40,000 troops by the end of the year.

KEY:
- Land war
- Air war
- Politics

KHE SANH

A US Air Force C-130 Hercules delivers much-needed supplies to Khe Sanh.

tactical target in the history of warfare. Around 10,000 communists died at a cost of 500 US marines. Some NVA units had losses of 90 percent. The NVA's legendary commander, General Giap, almost lost his life when 36 B-52 bombers pounded his field headquarters after US intelligence intercepts revealed that a high-ranking official was in the area.

Westmoreland's Gamble

Khe Sanh was relieved by April 1968, but in June it was abandoned. Westmoreland had taken a huge gamble over a position that was soon dispensed with anyway. The gamble had paid off, but if Khe Sanh had fallen, US involvement in Vietnam would have been in ruins.

Relief of Khe Sanh

The US marines initiated an operation to relieve the siege of Khe Sanh on April 1, 1968. Two battalions moved down Route 9 from the east, supported by three brigades of Air Cavalry. Their landing zones came under fire, but an NVA counterattack failed. By April 8, the road was clear. An Air Cavalry trooper hung up a sign at the base proclaiming: "Under new management."

Smoke and dust cover Khe Sanh during a rocket attack.

November 19 North Vietnam A US raid to free American POWs held in North Vietnam fails as the North Vietnamese move prisoners before the attack.

December

December 3 South Vietnam The US military presence reaches its lowest total in Vietnam since October 29, 1966, at 349,700 troops.

Tet Offensive

The Tet Offensive did not give the North Vietnamese the decisive victory they hoped for, but it shattered America's confidence in its ability to prevail in the Vietnam War.

Soldiers of the US 5th Marine Regiment take shelter behind a wall in Hue.

Timeline
1971 January–June

January 6 South Vietnam US secretary of defense Melvin R. Laird says that Vietnamization is working well; combat missions by US troops will end by the following summer.

January South Vietnam Enemy activity is apparently in decline.

February 8 Laos South Vietnamese troops have gone into Laos; no US troops have gone in at this stage.

April 7 United States As a further sign that the ground role of US forces is over, President Nixon announces more troop cuts.

KEY:
- Land war
- Air war
- Politics

Tet Offensive

Tet is the Vietnamese New Year festival. It lasts for seven days and is a time when many Vietnamese travel home to be near their families. In the first years of the Vietnam War, Tet was marked by a truce. In 1968, that changed.

Caught Unprepared

The Tet Offensive in 1968 took everyone by surprise. There were some signs that a major offensive was on its way, but the US military command expected fighting in the North. President Nguyen Van Thieu was on vacation. Staff at the State Department Vietnam desk in Washington were on leave.

A Tragic Miscalculation

Until January 1968, most of the fighting had taken place in the countryside. Tet would take it to the cities. City hotels were full of people from the countryside for the holiday, and in the relatively relaxed atmosphere, it was easy to infiltrate guerrillas and their weapons.

TARGETS IN THE TET OFFENSIVE

↑ Major towns attacked during the Tet Offensive.

Timeline

January 27, 1968 The supposed seven-day cease-fire for the Tet holiday begins.

January 29, 1968 The Allied cease-fire for Tet begins.

January 30, 1968 In predawn assaults, the North Vietnamese Army (NVA) and Viet Cong launch attacks throughout South Vietnam. This marks the start of the Tet Offensive.

January 31, 1968 Viet Cong troops attack the US Embassy in Saigon and seize the building. They hold part of it for six hours. US Marine Corps embassy guards and US Army military policemen retake the building. They kill all enemy soldiers in the embassy.

February 1, 1968 US forces successfully defend the city of Quang Tri. Operation Hue City to retake the city starts. It will see some of the heaviest fighting of the Vietnam War.

(continued, page 28)

April 7–12 South Vietnam US troops launch the five-day Operation Scott Orchard as a demonstration of continuing support for their South Vietnamese ally.

May 3–4 United States Marines are sent to Washington, DC, to help police control antiwar protesters.

May 12 South Vietnam Operation Imperial Lake, the last major US Marine Corps operation in Vietnam, takes place.

June 21 South Vietnam US troops continue to leave Vietnam; some 244,900 troops now remain in the country.

June

The Vietnam War

Timeline (continued)

February 9, 1968 Units of III Marine Amphibious Force beat back 2nd NVA Division's offensive at Da Nang.

February 24, 1968 Marines and ARVN troops finally wrest control of the ancient Citadel in Hue City from the NVA.

February 25, 1968 American forces finally declare the city of Hue secure.

February 29, 1968 Extra American troops arrive to prevent defeat in Hue.

March 2, 1968 Operation Hue City ends successfully as the 1st and 5th Marines defeat the NVA assault. Casualties include 142 marines and 1,943 enemy killed.

US marines search for snipers while fighting in Hue.

Tanks search for North Vietnamese forces in the Dong Ha area in the aftermath of Tet.

On the evening of January 30, 1968, simultaneous attacks began in 100 South Vietnamese cities and towns. The targets included not only the capital, Saigon, but also Da Nang, Hoi An, and Qui Nhon, coastal enclaves thought to be beyond the reach of the communists. Even the mountain resort of Dalat, previously spared by tacit agreement, was stormed.

In most places, the offensive was rapidly put down. But the

Timeline
1971 July–December

July 12 South Vietnam US troop strength now stands at 236,000; around 14,000 troops are leaving each month.

October 3 South Vietnam Nguyen Van Thieu's reelection as president is marked by protests and Viet Cong attacks.

July — October

July 9 South Vietnam US troops are no longer obligated to defend the region south of the DMZ.

August 18 South Vietnam Australia and New Zealand announce the withdrawal of their troops from Southeast Asia.

KEY:
 Land war
 Air war
 Politics

communists controlled the old imperial capital of Hue for 25 days. More than 4,000 communists in small teams attacked Saigon. A 19-man suicide squad seized the compound of the US Embassy. They held it for 6½ hours, to the horror of Americans watching the battle live on TV.

Televised Brutality

US audiences were shocked to see grinning South Vietnamese soldiers searching bodies for valuables. Many people, including the influential TV anchor Walter Cronkite, concluded that if, after three years of war, the United States could not protect its own embassy, it would never be able to hold the country.

In military terms, the Tet Offensive was a failure. The huge NVA losses (up to 50,000, compared with 2,000 Americans and 4,000 South Vietnamese soldiers) undoubtedly affected their morale. However, the offensive had sent a shockwave through the US military and public.

↑ The old imperial city of Hue was devastated during the Tet Offensive.

The Battle for the Citadel

The bitterest battle of Tet and one of the worst atrocities of the war took place around the Citadel in Hue. Communist forces armed with lists of names searched for government officials, doctors, merchants, teachers, clergymen, and foreigners. They found and murdered 2,800 people. Some were mutilated, others buried alive in mass graves. Nearly 150 US marines, 400 South Vietnamese, and 5,000 communists also died.

November 12 United States President Nixon declares that US forces now have only a defensive role in Vietnam.

November 26 North Vietnam As North Vietnam stalls over peace talks, President Nixon authorizes more bombing of North Vietnam.

December 31 South Vietnam To date, some 45,626 Americans have been killed in Vietnam.

December

The Death Toll Mounts

The Tet Offensive proved the turning point in the Vietnam War, but there was still more fighting to come. At home, Americans continued to protest against the war.

Helicopters lay a smokescreen during Operation Lamar Plain.

Timeline 1972 January–June

KEY:
- Land war
- Air war
- Politics

January 25 South Vietnam A new peace initiative is announced by Presidents Nixon and Nguyen Van Thieu to bring the war to an end.

February 21 China President Nixon becomes the first US president to visit China; he asks for help ending the war.

March 10 Cambodia US ally Lon Nol declares himself president.

March 10 South Vietnam The last American division, the US 101st Airborne, leaves Vietnam.

March 23 France Paris peace talks are suspended.

March 30 South Vietnam The North Vietnamese launch major offensive into South Vietnam, known as the Easter Offensive.

After blunting the Tet Offensive, US forces went after the enemy in an all-out attack, which General Westmoreland hoped would put the enemy on the defensive. Politically, however, 1968 was a period of disengagement for the United States. President Johnson halted the bombing of North Vietnam. The president announced not only that was he willing to discuss peace with North Vietnam's leaders but also that, much to his country's surprise, he would not seek reelection.

Heavy Losses

Although the Tet Offensive had broken the spirit of the Johnson administration, militarily the NVA and VC took heavy losses. The NVA failed to take Khe Sanh or Hue City. For the Viet Cong, Tet was even more damaging. The bulk of its cadres (trained leaders) died in major assaults against Saigon, Hue City, and other US military bases.

Timeline

March 16, 1968 US troops massacre more than 300 civilians in My Lai village.

October 31, 1968 President Johnson announces a complete halt in the aerial and naval bombardment of North Vietnam.

November 1, 1968 North Vietnamese officials announce they will meet in Paris with representatives from the United States, South Vietnam, and the Viet Cong to begin peace talks.

November 5, 1968 Richard Nixon is elected US president on a platform of "peace with honor" in Vietnam.

December 29, 1968 United States and South Vietnam announce they will not honor any holiday truces.

(continued, page 32)

← A tank of A Troop, 3rd Squadron, US 25th Infantry Division, on reconnaissance.

April 7 North Vietnam As the Easter Offensive continues, US aircraft resume bombing in North Vietnam.

May 4 France Peace talks are suspended indefinitely.

May — June

April 15–20 United States A wave of protests sweeps university campuses across the United States.

May 8 North Vietnam The US Navy bombs Haiphong and other North Vietnamese harbors.

Timeline (continued)

February 16, 1969 Allied forces observe 24-hour cease-fire during Tet. Both Viet Cong and NVA forces break the truce at least 203 times.

February 23, 1969 Communist forces launch attacks against US targets across South Vietnam.

May 10, 1969 Operation Apache Snow sees US paratroopers capture the heavily protected Hamburger Hill, named for the amount of blood spilled on it.

September 2, 1969 The president of North Vietnam, Ho Chi Minh, dies.

November 1, 1969 Operation Toan Thang is launched; it results in 5,493 communist deaths.

December 1, 1969 The first drawing of the highly unpopular US draft lottery takes place.

A US howitzer crew fires a shell.

Despite such losses, North Vietnam nevertheless saw the Tet Offensive and its aftermath as the "beginning of the end" of its quest to unify the country.

The War in 1969

There was still a lot of hard fighting to do in Vietnam. U.S. military strength in South Vietnam peaked at 539,000 men and women before a gradual reduction began. The United States had to train its allies in the Army of the Republic of Vietnam (ARVN) to assume more of the fighting as its own forces began a slow but steady process of redeployment.

Despite the announced withdrawal of US forces, the fighting on the ground not only continued, but the tempo of operations actually increased. Both sides were

Timeline
1972 July–December

July 13 France Peace talks resume after a 10-week break.

September 16 South Vietnam With massive support from US aircraft, the South is now defeating the Easter Offensive.

October 8 France At the peace talks, a breakthrough occurs when North Vietnam agrees to the continuing existence of South Vietnam.

KEY:
- Land war
- Air war
- Politics

The Death Toll Mounts

← US marines of the 2nd Battalion, 9th Marine Regiment, relax before operations begin.

eager to position themselves for the approaching fresh peace negotiations, which started again in Paris in early 1969 as a new US president entered office.

Determined to achieve "peace with honor," President Richard M. Nixon and his national security advisor, Henry Kissinger, reassured South Vietnamese president Nguyen Van Thieu that the United States would not "cut and run" in its commitment to defend South Vietnam against communist aggression. In private, however, both American politicians sought disengagement from an unpopular war that continued to take hundreds of US lives.

My Lai Massacre

In March 1968, American troops killed 300 people—mostly women and children—in the village of My Lai, South Vietnam. The soldiers also burnt the village, angry that many of their comrades had been killed and injured in the area. When the US public learned about My Lai in November 1969, many questioned the conduct of US soldiers in Vietnam. The soldiers' leader, Lieutenant William Calley, was tried and given a life sentence for the killings but was released in 1974.

November 7 United States Nixon is reelected president of the United States.

November 11 South Vietnam Direct US participation in the Vietnam War ends.

December 13 France Talks between US secretary of state Henry Kissinger and North Vietnamese negotiator Le Duc Tho stall again.

December 18 North Vietnam As talks stall, President Nixon orders air attacks against Hanoi and Haiphong.

December

Operation Rolling Thunder

Begun in March 1965 and continued until November 1968, Operation Rolling Thunder (ORT) was a US and South Vietnamese bombing campaign against North Vietnam.

US Air Force F-105 Thunderchiefs drop 750-lb bombs on NVA targets in December. →→

Timeline 1973 January–June

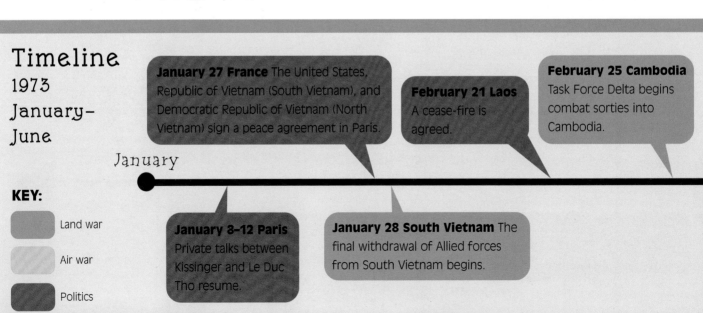

January 3–12 Paris Private talks between Kissinger and Le Duc Tho resume.

January 27 France The United States, Republic of Vietnam (South Vietnam), and Democratic Republic of Vietnam (North Vietnam) sign a peace agreement in Paris.

January 28 South Vietnam The final withdrawal of Allied forces from South Vietnam begins.

February 21 Laos A cease-fire is agreed.

February 25 Cambodia Task Force Delta begins combat sorties into Cambodia.

KEY:
- Land war
- Air war
- Politics

Operation Rolling Thunder

← An F-4 drops Mk 84 laser-guided bombs over North Vietnam in 1971.

Since the start of the war, US military planners had been eager to bomb North Vietnamese tactical targets such as railroads. The administration in Washington, DC, however, was concerned about the effect of civilian casualties on public opinion at home and on its allies overseas. When the military pressure paid off and Operation Rolling Thunder began, the government had to approve all targets. Bombing was forbidden within 10 miles (16 km) of the capital, Hanoi, for example, to protect civilian life.

The Campaign Lengthens

Rolling Thunder was intended as a short campaign that would demonstrate US air superiority. In 1964, US planners still hoped that it would make North Vietnam abandon its support for communist guerrillas and discuss peace terms. But that initial aim failed, and the campaign lasted three and a half years.

Timeline

August 5, 1964 President Johnson orders first air strikes against North Vietnamese targets.

February 13, 1965 President Johnson authorizes the start of the rolling air attacks on North Vietnamese targets. The first air strikes hit the Ho Chi Minh Trail.

March 1965 US Navy joins Operation Rolling Thunder (ORT) when aircraft from carriers USS *Hancock* and USS *Ranger* attack Phu Qui ammunition depot.

December 15, 1965 US Air Force aircraft destroy a North Vietnamese power plant at Uongbi. This is the first US air raid on a major North Vietnamese industrial target.

(continued, page 36)

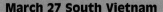

March — June

June 13 France The United States, South Vietnam, and North Vietnam sign a starting agreement that puts the Paris Peace Accord into effect; peace seems to have come to Vietnam.

March 27 South Vietnam This is the last day of the 60-day cease-fire during which US POWs have been released.

The Vietnam War

Timeline (continued)

July 20, 1967 A revised ORT target list is issued. It permits air attacks on 16 additional fixed targets and 23 road, rail, and waterway segments inside the restricted Hanoi-Haiphong area.

August 2, 1967 Hanoi's Paul Doumer rail and highway bridge is hit for the first time. The center span is knocked down and two others damaged.

August 13-19, 1967 Bridges, bypasses, rail yards, and military storage areas are bombed in an effort to sever communications between Hanoi and Haiphong, the most important deepwater port in the North.

October 25, 1967 Paul Doumer bridge hit again.

December 19, 1967 Rebuilt center span of Paul Doumer bridge knocked out again.

October 31, 1968 Operation Rolling Thunder is halted after failing to achieve its goals.

Explosions on the ground during Operation Colorado just north of Tam Ky.

As Rolling Thunder went on, the raids grew in size and intensity. US bombers flew missions from bases in Thailand or from aircraft carriers off Vietnam. The missions' aims also changed. The Americans now aimed to demoralize the North Vietnamese civilian population. The United States also wanted to destroy North Vietnam's infrastructure to make it more difficult for the North to send troops and equipment into the South. Neither aim was particularly successful.

Problems for Pilots

US pilots faced serious problems. Most had been trained for nuclear warfare, not conventional bombing raids. North Vietnam's air defenses had modern ground-to-air

Timeline
1973 July–December

KEY:
- Land war
- Air war
- Politics

July 1 United States The new financial year sees US aid to Vietnam massively reduced.

July 30 South Vietnam Fewer than 250 US military personnel are now in South Vietnam.

August United States A US district court rules that the secret war in Cambodia is unconstitutional.

August 14 United States Congress declares the end of US-funded military actions in Southeast Asia.

Operation Rolling Thunder

artillery from China and the Soviet Union. Its pilots flew slow but highly maneuverable Soviet MiG fighters. By November 1968, an estimated 864,000 tons (784,000 tonnes) of explosives had been dropped on North Vietnam (compared to about 500,000 tons [454,000 tonnes] in the Pacific Theater of World War II). Yet Rolling Thunder had achieved none of its goals. The operation was therefore quietly abandoned.

↑ Phosphorus bombs explode during Operation Georgia.

Losing the War at Home

As the 1960s wore on, middle America underwent a shift in its opinion toward Vietnam. At the start, Americans mostly supported military action. By the end of the decade, the majority had turned against it. The Tet Offensive of January 1968 dealt a huge blow to public confidence in America's ability to defeat its enemy. For the first time, it looked as if the United States might not win the war.

← A flight of B-52 Stratofortress bombers drop their bombs.

October United States In response to the invasion of Cambodia, Congress passes the War Powers Act limiting the president's power to wage war.

October

December

December 15 South Vietnam A Joint Military Commission unit is ambushed by communist troops, and a US soldier is killed.

Cambodia

Cambodia's fortunes fell with the Vietnam War. Its political instability allowed the rise of the Khmer Rouge regime that would devastate the country and its people.

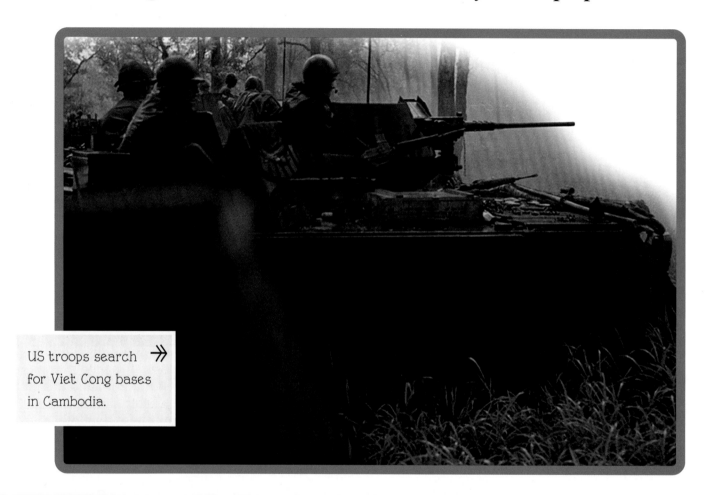

US troops search for Viet Cong bases in Cambodia.

Timeline
1974 January–June

February 21 United States A report claims that the use of defoliants will damage Vietnam for up to a century.

March 22 South Vietnam The Viet Cong propose a new truce with the United States and South Vietnam.

April 27–May 2 South Vietnam The ARVN stages its last major offensive against the North Vietnamese at Svay Rieng.

KEY:
- Land war
- Air war
- Politics

Cambodia

Like Vietnam and Laos, Cambodia was part of French Indochina. When the French left in 1954, Prince Sihanouk, hereditary ruler of Cambodia, was recognized as the legitimate authority. As trouble brewed in neighboring Vietnam, he courted first the United States, then the North Vietnamese, and then the United States again. North Vietnam, however, used bases over the Cambodian border to provide supplies to its allies in South Vietnam. The supplies were moved southward along the so-called Ho Chi Minh Trail, a network of routes along the Vietnam-Cambodia border.

Cambodia Is Bombed

When President Nixon came to power in early 1969, he proposed a secret bombing campaign against Vietnamese strongholds in Cambodia and the Ho Chi Minh Trail. Sihanouk's military supplied the intelligence for the raids, which continued for 14 months. The bombing strayed into inhabited areas, however, and Cambodians died in the raids. As casualties rose, the country became destabilized.

Timeline

1954 French colonial rulers finally leave Cambodia; Prince Norodom Sihanouk is recognized as the country's ruler.

March 19, 1970 General Lon Nol, Sihanouk's prime minister, siezes power in a US-backed bloodless coup.

April 29, 1970 South Vietnamese and US Army forces carry out search-and-destroy operations in a dozen base areas in Cambodia. They are looking to destroy the Ho Chi Minh Trail that allows supplies to be smuggled into South Vietnam by the North Vietnamese. US boats sweep up the Mekong Delta to reopen a supply line to Phnom Penh, the Cambodian capital.

(continued, page 40)

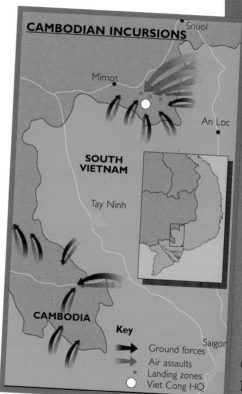

← The Cambodian incursions in 1970 disrupted communist plans to a limited degree.

May 9 United States Congress begins impeachment proceedings against President Richard Nixon.

May 16 South Vietnam At the Battle of the Iron Triangle, an NVA division takes control of An Dien and continues its advance south.

June US Marine Anthony Lukeman becomes chief of the Vietnamese Marine Corps.

Timeline (continued)

April 30, 1970 The US and South Vietnamese invasion of Cambodia sparks a public outcry in the United States.

May 4, 1970 As raids into Cambodia continue, US college campuses witness a wave of antiwar protests; at Kent State University in Kent, Ohio, National Guardsmen shoot and kill four student demonstrators.

June 27, 1970 The last US and South Vietnamese soldiers leave Cambodia; some 4,764 enemy have been killed while US casualties are 399 killed and 1,501 wounded.

April 1, 1975 General Lon Nol flees to the United States.

April 17, 1975 Khmer Rouge, led by Pol Pot, enter Phnom Penh; their hardline communist reign will see two million Cambodians killed in the next three years.

A Bloodless Coup

In March 1970, Prime Minister Lon Nol staged a bloodless, US-backed coup. In Beijing, Sihanouk set up a government of national unity that included the hardline communists of the Khmer Rouge. The Khmers' leader, Pol Pot, used North Vietnamese military strength to establish Khmer power on the ground. By 1973, he had built an army of 40,000 followers.

The Khmer Rouge

When the United States left Vietnam in the 1970s, the NVA pulled out of Cambodia, leaving the Khmer Rouge in control. The Cambodian government fled. On April 17, 1975, the Khmer Rouge entered the capital, Phnom Penh.

Pol Pot believed that, in order to build a perfect communist society, everyone had to become a peasant. He drove people from the cities into the countryside and killed anyone with any education or professional skill; even people who wore spectacles were murdered. The result was that little worked.

↑ US helicopters prepare to leave on a mission into Cambodia, May 14, 1970.

Timeline
1974 July–December

July 1 United States US aid to South Vietnam continues to fall.

August 8 United States Caught up in the Watergate scandal, President Nixon is forced to resign from office.

August 9 United States Vice President Gerald R. Ford succeeds Nixon as president.

July — October

KEY:
- Land war
- Air war
- Politics

Cambodia

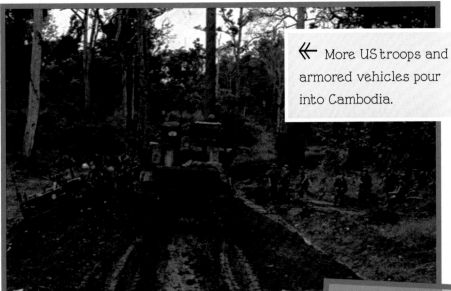

← More US troops and armored vehicles pour into Cambodia.

Ho Chi Minh Trail

The trail was a system of mountain and jungle paths and trails used by North Vietnam to infiltrate troops and supplies into South Vietnam, Cambodia, and Laos. It took more than one month's march to travel from North to South Vietnam. By the late 1960s, the trail was wide enough for heavy trucks in places. By 1974, it had some paved roads and underground support facilities, such as hospitals and fuel-storage tanks.

Without trained engineers, dams and irrigation projects built by hand failed. Hundreds of thousands of people who escaped execution starved to death. The Khmer Rouge were thought to be responsible for the deaths of two million of their own people.

In 1978, the Vietnamese moved in to stop the killing. The United States had not yet normalized relations with Hanoi, however, so along with many other countries, it condemned the Vietnamese invasion.

← US and South Vietnamese efforts to close the trail failed.

December

December 13 South Vietnam The North Vietnamese Army begins a new offensive against the South to conquer it; the NVA is supplied by the Soviet Union.

December 31 South Vietnam NVA units encircle Phuoc Long City close to the Cambodian border.

End Game

As the war grew more unpopular in the United States, US troops were withdrawn from South Vietnam. The war finally ended with a communist victory.

A US AH-1 Cobra gunship in South Vietnam. Its narrow shape let it hide in the trees. →→

Timeline
1975
January–
March

January

January 7 South Vietnam
The NVA captures Phuoc Long province.

KEY:

 Land war

 Air war

 Politics

End Game

As the South Vietnamese took on more military duties from the Americans, the US casualty rate fell. Meanwhile, however, the air war continued to inflict casualties on the enemy. By the end of 1970, US and South Vietnamese aircraft had disrupted North Vietnam's ability to launch further Tet-style offensives.

Allied Successes

The success of the Allied tactics against communist sanctuaries in Laos and Cambodia, and a campaign against the Ho Chi Minh Trail, forced the North Vietnamese to revert to guerrilla-style tactics. Such tactics, used in the early 1960s, now failed. Pacification efforts by US marines and the Army of the Republic of Vietnam (ARVN) helped turn South Vietnamese peasants against the communists. The North Vietnamese Army (NVA) and Viet Cong (VC) attacks on villages increased. Combined US and ARVN pressure ensured that the NVA was kept on the defensive throughout 1970.

Timeline

February 17, 1970 President Nixon states that the South Vietnamese will take a greater role in fighting, a process known as Vietnamization.

April 29, 1970 South Vietnamese and US forces carry out search-and-destroy operations in Cambodia, prompting a public outcry in the United States.

February 8, 1971 South Vietnamese troops enter Laos.

May 12, 1971 Operation Imperial Lake is the last major US Marine Corps operation in Vietnam.

March 30, 1972 A major North Vietnamese offensive, the Easter Offensive, begins.

(continued, page 44)

← Private Edward Sellere, US 25th Infantry Division, prepares for a mission.

March

March 10 South Vietnam The NVA attacks Ban Me Thuot at the start of the 1975 Spring Offensive.

March 19 South Vietnam The South Vietnamese army abandons Quang Tri City and its province.

March 24 South Vietnam Quang Ngai City and Tam Ky fall to advancing NVA; next day, they capture Hue City.

March 26 South Vietnam The NVA capture the former Marine Corps base at Chu Lai.

March 30 South Vietnam The NVA enters Da Nang City and captures the Da Nang Air Base.

Timeline (continued)

April 7, 1972 US bombing of North Vietnam resumes.

December 18, 1972 After peace talks stall again, Nixon orders air attacks against Hanoi and Haiphong.

January 27-28, 1973 Peace agreement finally signed in Paris; the next day, final withdrawal of Allied forces from South Vietnam begins.

December 13, 1974 NVA begins a new offensive against South Vietnam.

April 29, 1975 US marines evacuate civilians from Saigon.

April 30, 1975 NVA enters Saigon; the conflict is over.

When North Vietnam stalled at the Paris Peace Talks, Nixon resumed bombings. →

A Temporary Lull

As the United States turned its attention to ending the war and addressing domestic political problems brought on by the Watergate scandal (1973–1974), Hanoi launched a major offensive during March and April 1972, known as the "Easter Offensive." Supported by US ground advisors and aircraft flying nonstop strikes against waves of North Vietnamese tanks and armored vehicles, the Army of the Republic of Vietnam (ARVN) put up a spirited defense. It later began offensive operations that forced its enemy to seek an armistice. Determined to be reelected and end the war, President Nixon and his national security advisor, Henry Kissinger, used both force and diplomacy in their bid to end the conflict. After a massive bombing campaign against Hanoi during Christmas 1972, the United States introduced an uneasy lull in the war during 1973.

Fall of the South

Between 1971 and 1974, the bulk of US ground and air forces departed South Vietnam and turned the war over to the ARVN. The Paris

Timeline
1975
April

April

April 21 South Vietnam President Nguyen Van Thieu resigns and flees to Taiwan.

April 17 Cambodia The capital, Phnom Penh, falls to forces of the Khmer Rouge.

KEY:
 Land war
 Air war
 Politics

End Game

↑ As US forces withdrew, the burden of the fighting fell on the soldiers of the South.

Peace Accords signed in January 1973 seemed to guarantee the survival of South Vietnam, but the communists had no intention of ending the war. They sensed that victory was close. Each side accused the other of violating the truce. Fighting therefore continued. But with the withdrawal of US forces, the South lacked air support to blunt the NVA. When the North launched a major offensive in early 1975, the ARVN crumbled and the NVA rolled into Saigon. The Vietnam War had ended in a communist victory.

The Final Flight

One of the most memorable images of the Vietnam War is the evacuation of people by helicopter from the roof of the US Embassy in Saigon as the city fell to the NVA. The collapse of the South was so quick that plans to evacuate civilians were thrown into disarray. Panic increased as American and Vietnamese fought desperately for a place on the last helicopters to leave Saigon before it fell.

← A memorial stands outside Saigon at the end of the war.

April 28 South Vietnam General Duong Van "Big" Minh becomes the last president of South Vietnam.

April 29 South Vietnam US marines carry out Operation Frequent Wind to evacuate Americans and other civilians from Saigon.

April 30 South Vietnam The NVA enters Saigon and arrests General Minh; South Vietnamese resistance collapses. The long conflict in Vietnam is over.

Glossary

ARVN Army of the Republic of Vietnam (South Vietnam).

cadre A small group of trained people who organize a larger movement.

Charlie US slang for the Viet Cong.

coup d'état A sudden, often violent, seizure of power over a state.

defoliant A chemical used to destroy vegetation that might be used as cover.

delta A low-lying triangular area formed where a river splits into many channels to enter a larger body of water.

DMZ The Demilitarized Zone, the dividing line between North and South Vietnam established in 1954 by the Geneva Convention.

domino effect A US political theory that if a country became communist, its neighbors were more likely to become communist in turn.

guerrilla A soldier who does not wear uniform and who operates behind enemy lines.

infiltration The penetration of enemy positions without being detected.

intelligence Secret information gathered by espionage.

intercept An intercepted enemy message.

marine A soldier serving on a ship or other naval installation.

NVA North Vietnamese Army.

offensive A coordinated series of military attacks.

sabotage Guerrilla attacks on enemy equipment and infrastructure.

search-and-destroy Describing operations in which troops go into the countryside to hunt for the enemy.

smokescreen A dense cloud of smoke used to hide military maneuvers.

truce A temporary cease-fire.

VC The Viet Cong, communist guerrillas operating in South Vietnam.

Viet Minh An armed independence movement in Vietnam in the 1950s.

Vietnamization A US policy of handing over fighting to the South Vietnamese.

Further Reading

Books

Britton, Tamara L. *The Vietnam Veterans Memorial* (Symbols, Landmarks, and Monuments). Checkerboard Books, 2004.

Caputo, Philip. *10,000 Days of Thunder: A History of the Vietnam War.* Atheneum, 2005.

Daynes, Katie. *The Vietnam War* (Usborne Young Reading). Usborne Books, 2008.

Gifford, Clive. *The Vietnam War* (How Did It Happen). Lucent, 2005.

Gitlin, Marty. *U.S. Involvement in Vietnam* (Essential Events). ABDO Publishing Company, 2010.

Mason, Andrew. *The Vietnam War: A Primary Source History* (In Their Own Words). Gareth Stevens Publishing, 2005.

Murray, Stuart. *Vietnam War* (DK Eyewitness Books). Dorling Kindersley, 2005.

O'Connell, Kim A. *Primary Source Accounts of the Vietnam War* (America's War Through Primary Sources). Myreportlinks.com, 2006.

Smith-Ilera, Danielle. *Vietnam POWs* (We the People). Compass Point Books, 2008.

Westwell, Ian. *The Vietnam War 1964–1975* (Wars Day by Day). Brown Bear Books, 2008.

Zeinert, Karen. *Valiant Women of the Vietnam War.* 21st Century, 2000.

Websites

www.vietnampix.com
A pictorial guide to the whole conflict.

www.pbs.org/battlefieldvietnam
PBS site about the battles of Vietnam.

http://vietnam.vassar.edu
Vassar College overview of the war, including North Vietnamese archive materials.

www.spartacus.schoolnet.co.uk/VietnamWar.htm
Overview of the Vietnam War.

www.historyplace.com/unitedstates/vietnam
History Place illustrated timeline of the conflict from 1945 to 1975.

www.pbs.org/wgbh/amex/vietnam
PBS American Experience site dedicated to Vietnam Online.

www.illyria.com/vnwomen.html
Women in the Vietnam War.

Index

AK-47 Kalashnikov assault rifle 17
antiwar movement 21
Army of the Republic of Vietnam (ARVN) 4, 13, 16, 32, 43, 44, 45
"brown water" navy 21
Buddhists 11
Calley, Lieutenant William 33
Cambodia 7, 38, 39, 40, 41, 43
China 4, 37
Cold War 4
coup d'état 11, 40
Dalat 28
Da Nang 17, 28
demilitarized zone (DMZ) 4, 12, 19, 23
Democratic Republic of Vietnam 9
Dien Bien Phu 8, 9, 24
domino theory 4, 9
Easter Offensive 44
France 4, 7, 8, 9, 39
Giap, General 25
"grunts" 17
guerrillas 4, 11, 13, 27, 35, 43
Gulf of Tonkin 12, 13
Haiphong 6
Hanoi 19, 35, 41, 44
helicopters 15, 16, 18, 30, 40, 45
Ho Chi Minh 8, 9
Ho Chi Minh Trail 15, 19, 20, 39, 41, 43
Hoi An 28
Hue 26, 28, 29, 31
I Corps Tactical Zone (ICTZ) 12, 19

Indochina 7, 8, 39
infantry 5, 17, 31, 43
Johnson, President Lyndon B. 11, 12, 21, 23, 31
Kennedy, President John F. 7, 9
Khe Sanh 17, 22, 23, 24, 25, 31
Khmer Rouge 38, 40, 41
Kissinger, Henry 33, 44
Laos 7, 16, 20, 23, 39, 41, 43
leathernecks 19
Lon Nol 40
marines 11, 12, 13, 14, 22, 23, 24, 25, 26, 28, 29, 33, 43
"McNamara Line" 19
Mekong Delta 16, 20, 21
Military Assistance Command, Vietnam (MACV) 11
"More Flags" campaign 21
My Lai Masssacre 33
Ngo Dinh Diem, President 11
Nguyen Van Thieu, President 27, 33
Nixon, President Richard M. 33, 39, 44
North Vietnamese Army (NVA) 13, 14, 17, 19, 22, 23, 24, 25, 29, 31, 34, 40, 43, 45
Operation Colorado 36
Operation Garfield 15
Operation Georgia 37
Operation Lamar Plain 30

Operation Market Time 16
Operation Niagara 24
Operation Rolling Thunder 12, 16, 34, 35, 36, 37
Paris Peace Accords 44–45
Paris Peace Talks 44
"peace with honor" 33
Phnom Penh 40
Pol Pot 40
protests 4, 21, 30
"punji stakes" 17
Qui Nhon 28
Republic of Vietnam 4, 9
RP-2s (rocket-propelled grenade launchers) 17
Saigon 19, 20, 28, 31, 45
search-and-destroy 15, 16
Sihanouk, Prince 39, 40
Southeast Asia 7
Soviet Union 4, 17, 37
Tet Offensive 26, 27, 28, 29, 30, 31, 32, 37, 43
Thailand 7, 21, 36
Tu Duc, Emperor 7
tunnels 20
US Air Force 16, 20, 25, 34
US Army 19
US Navy 16, 19, 20
USS *Maddox* 13
Viet Cong (VC) 4, 10, 11, 13, 14, 15, 16, 17, 18, 19, 31, 38, 43
Viet Minh 4, 6
Vietnamese New Year 27
Westmoreland, General William C. 11, 15, 23, 24, 25, 31